Word Family Stationery

By Marilyn Myers Burch

SCHOLASTIC
PROFESSIONAL BOOKS

NEW YORK • TORONTO • LONDON • AUCKLAND • SYDNEY
MEXICO CITY • NEW DELHI • HONG KONG

For my parents, Wilfried and Bernice Myers, who
encouraged me to begin writing at an early age.

Thank you to Deborah Schecter and Ingrid Blinken
at Scholastic. I appreciate all of your help and efforts.

Cover design by Jaime Lucero
Interior design by Solutions by Design, Inc.
Cover and interior art by Maxie Chambliss

ISBN: 0-439-12973-7

Contents

Introduction

Children's lives are full of magical moments. Take for example the moment when a child takes his first steps or says her first word. But of all the magical moments, none has quite the same meaning as the moment when a child realizes that he or she can read— that squiggled lines and dots and dashes represent letters that in turn join to form words. The same magic surrounds the moment when a child puts pen to paper and writes not zigzags or a string of random letters, but rather a series of letters that reflect a growing knowledge of sound-spelling relationships. While these moments are magical, young learners need not rely on magic or luck to make them real. Indeed, there is much that we as educators can do to help children in their quest to make meaning of the print they encounter and produce. While it is essential that we provide children with countless opportunities to read and write, we must also offer systematic and direct instruction in sound-spelling relationships to help them unlock the mysteries of print.

Phonics and Phonograms

Over the years there has been much debate over phonics instruction. What is important to remember is that phonics instruction is not an end in and of itself, but rather a means to the end of children's learning to read and write. While teachers and researchers have argued about just how much phonics instruction children need, it has become clear that all children benefit from some direct phonics instruction. It is a fact that once children have developed a strong understanding of sound-spelling relationships, they are able to decode texts with greater ease, thus freeing them to focus on the meaning of the piece and the joys of reading.

One way to help children become lifelong readers and writers is to introduce them to *phonograms*. Phonograms, also referred to as word families or rimes, are letters that stand for a sound or a series of sounds. For example, the letters *ack* stand for the sounds /a/ and /k/. Words such as *tack*, *back*, and *sack* all contain the same phonogram; put another way, they all belong to the same word family. In her book *Beginning to Read: Thinking and Learning About Print* (1990), researcher Marilyn Adams reported that of the 286 phonograms that appear in primary grade texts, 95% of them were pronounced the same in every word in which they appeared. So, once children learn a phonogram they can begin to recognize and generate a large number of words from the same family with ease and accuracy.

How to Use This Book

The stationery pages that follow are designed to reinforce children's recognition of phonograms while building on their growing concepts of the functions of print. Each of the reproducible stationery sheets highlights one of 40 phonograms drawn from high-utility lists. Each shaped sheet represents a word containing the chosen phonogram. The shape gives children a visual clue as they read the first word that appears in the word bank and then go on to identify and record other words from the same family.

While you and your students are bound to come up with many creative ways of using the reproducible sheets as part of your reading and writing program, what follows are a few suggestions to get you started:

USING WORD FAMILY STATIONERY

Word Work

While there is no right or wrong way to introduce children to phonograms and this stationery, you might want to begin your exploration of word families with a session of word work. A word work mini-lesson for the phonogram -*at* might go something like this:

1. Gather children around you. Write the letters of the phonogram on a sheet of chart paper and ask if someone can tell you what sounds these letters stand for.

2. On the next line, write the word *cat* and draw or display a labeled picture of a cat. Blend the word out loud, running your finger under each letter. Have a volunteer come up and underline the letters *at* and repeat what sounds they stand for.

3. Distribute a stationery sheet to each child with the word bank cut off. Ask children if they can think of other words that have the /at/ sound.

4. Invite children to blend and then record the words on their stationery sheets as you record their suggestions on the chart paper. After students have generated a list of five to ten words, reread the list together.

You might have children include these pages in personal word work binders that they can refer to while doing their own writing. Or, use the chart paper to start a word wall. Simply post the chart paper along with a pen in a spot that children can reach. Invite them to add any other words from the same word family that they can find. Be sure to set aside a time for children to share these new words with the class and to copy them into their word work binders as well.

Sound Scavenger Hunt

Help build children's curiosity about words with a sound scavenger hunt. Invite students to search your room for objects whose names belong to the word family highlighted on their stationery sheet. For example, if you challenge children to find words containing the -*ock* phonogram they might find a clock, a block, a sock, etc. Have children start out by looking for the words in the word box. Then, challenge them to find more words from the same family to add to their stationery sheets.

Extension: Encourage children to continue acting as word detectives after the school day is over by sending them on an environmental print scavenger hunt. Using their stationery pages, children can look for signs, advertisements, food cartons, and so on that have words containing the phonogram you are studying. Have children share their findings with the class the next day.

Cat, Sat, Plate!

Once children have been able to identify several words in a phonogram family, invite them to play this phonogram-based version of "Duck, Duck, Goose." Here children go around the circle saying words whose names include the same phonogram such as *bat*, *mat*, *rat*. Rather than say *goose*, players say a word from another word family before racing around the circle.

Musical Word Match

1. Make a series of onset and rime cards that can be paired to make words. (Onsets are the consonants that come before a vowel in a syllable such as *gr* in grapes. Rime refers to the vowels that follow the onset such as *apes* in grapes.)You'll need some lively music as well.

2. Distribute a card to each child in the class. Be

sure that each card can be combined with another to make a word.

3. Challenge children to find a classmate whose card has a word part that they can combine with their own to make a word while the music is still playing.

4. Stop the music and ask children who have found a partner to share their word with the rest of the class. Write their words on a piece of chart paper. If you'd like, you can ask these children to sit out as other students search for pairs. Or, you can have the whole class try to come up with some new words once the music starts again.

Match and Sort

1. Pair up the *-unk/-ack*, and *-ink/-ock* pages to play a matching and sorting game. Start by cutting the word bank off each page.

2. Post the stationery on a sheet of chart paper or the chalkboard. (Note: For this activity, you may want to use a copier to enlarge the stationery sheets before you post them.)

3. Next, using magazine pictures, pictures from old workbooks, or stickers, make picture cards for words in each word family. For example, if you were making cards for the phonograms *-ink* and *-ock*, you might prepare cards with pictures of a skating rink, a bottle of ink, a rock, a clock, a block, and so on.

4. Hold up each card and challenge children to identify the picture and to tell you which word family it belongs to. Invite children to label the illustrations and then paste them to the corresponding sheet of stationery.

If...Then

Use the stationery sheets to introduce children to unfamiliar words and the important skill of decoding by analogy. Once children have had a chance to familiarize themselves with a few words from a given word family, invite them to use their knowledge to identify new words. For example, if you were using the *-ale* page you might introduce the word *stale* in the following way:

1. Write *stale* on a sheet of chart paper or the chalkboard. Write the word *whale* below it. On the next two lines write sentences using each word *(The bread was so stale and hard we could not eat it. The big blue whale swam in the ocean all day long.)*.

2. Invite children to read the word *whale* first. Then ask them to find the same phonogram in the word *stale*.

3. Next, ask children to use that information along with their knowledge of the *-ale* phonogram to decode the new word. You might begin by saying "If W-H-A-L-E is whale, than S-T-A-L-E must be. . ." Or, pointing to the word *stale*, you might want to say, "This word has *st* like stop and *-ale* like whale. If I put the sounds together I get stale, st—ale, stale." Have children check their answers using the context clues offered in the sentences. Ask: *Does your answer make sense? How do you know?*

Silly Stories & Tricky Tongue Twisters

Children love silly stories and rollicking rhymes, but often it is difficult for them to make sense of stories that have a high proportion of rhyming phonograms. Rather than give children the task of decoding these texts, invite them to write their own tongue twisters, rhymes or silly stories. Children can use the stationery shapes and word banks as inspirations for their writing. For example, they might use the *-ice* stationery page to write a rhyme about a family of mice.

Word Family Albums

1. Distribute a stationery sheet to each child in the class. Once you have reviewed the highlighted sound-spelling relationship, explain that you are going to create a collaborative word family album.

2. Invite each child to find a new word that contains the same phonogram. Then, have children write the word on one line of their stationery sheet.

3. On another line have them write a short sentence using their word.

4. Have children draw an illustration to accompany their sentence on a separate sheet of unlined paper.

5. Ask a volunteer to create a cover for your album using another copy of the stationery sheet. Next, bind the cover and the students' pages using a stapler, or if you would prefer, a hole punch and yarn. For a shaped album, you or your students can cut the pages out along the lines of the stationery shape. If you were creating an -*og* family album for example, you could make the album in the shape of a dog.

Helpful Hints

◎ The unlined paper that students use for their illustrations must be small enough to fit on the stationery sheet once the children have written their words and sentences. You may want to precut some paper. You can also use a copier to enlarge the stationery sheets in order to give more room for children's art.

◎ You may want to paste the pages to oaktag or laminate them before binding to give your album added durability.

Stationery for Any Occasion

While the stationery pages were designed to help children recognize phonograms, they can add flair to many of your classroom communications and your curriculum. For example, you might use the *-ake* page to create an invitation to a class birthday celebration. If you are studying whales, you might distribute copies of the *-ale* page for students to record whale facts. The *-uck* (truck) or the *-ain* (train) pages could complement a study of transportation.

Here are other high-utility phonograms you may want to review with your class:

-ab	-age	-am	-ave
cab	cage	clam	brave
dab	page	dam	crave
drab	rage	ham	gave
grab	stage	jam	pave
lab	wage	slam	save
nab		swam	wave

-eak	-ear	-eat	-ent
beak	clear	eat	bent
leak	dear	heat	cent
peak	fear	meat	dent
speak	hear	neat	rent
squeak	near	seat	sent
	year	treat	tent

-ill	-it	-oat	-ob
drill	bit	boat	cob
fill	fit	coat	knob
hill	hit	goat	mob
pill	kit	throat	rob
spill	pit		sob
will	sit		

-oke	-ope	-ore	-um
choke	cope	bore	drum
joke	hope	core	glum
poke	mope	more	gum
smoke	rope	score	hum
spoke		store	plum
woke		wore	sum

Word Bank | **backpack** black rack snack tack track

Word Bank | **pail** mail nail snail tail trail

WORD FAMILY -ain

Word Bank | train brain chain drain main rain

Word Family Stationery Scholastic Professional Books

Word Bank | **cake** lake make rake snake take

Word Family Stationery   Scholastic Professional Books

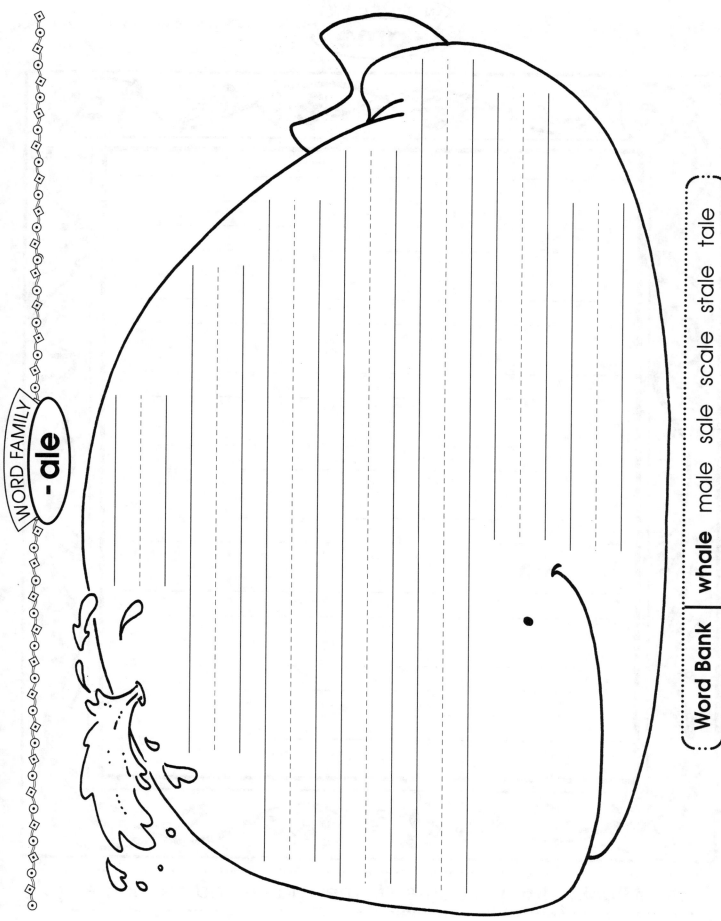

WORD FAMILY
-ale

Word Bank whale male sale scale stale tale

Word Bank | **frame** came flame game name same

Word Family Stationery   Scholastic Professional Books

Word Bank | pan can fan man ran van

Word Family Stationery   Scholastic Professional Books

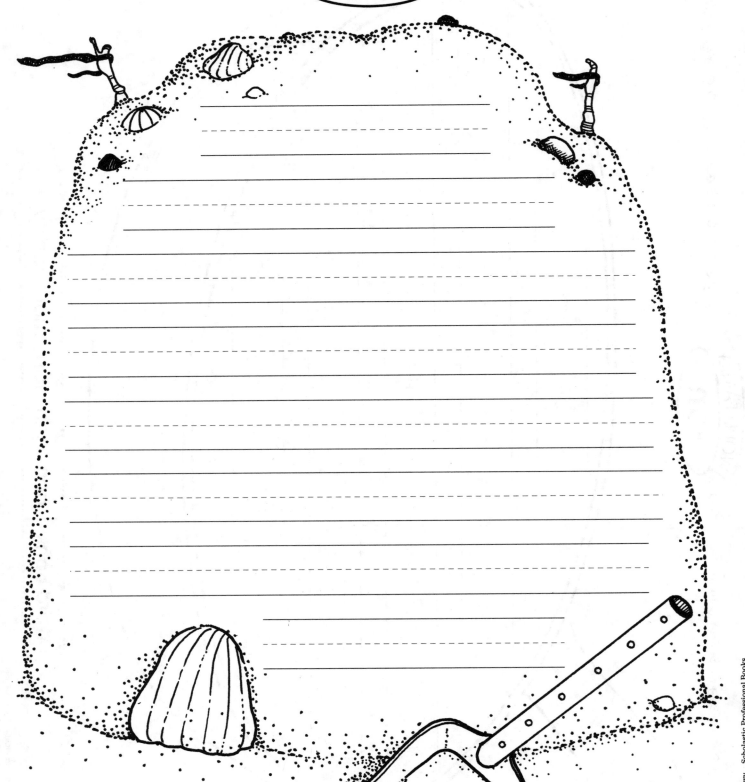

Word Bank | **sand** and band hand land stand

Word Family Stationery Scholastic Professional Books

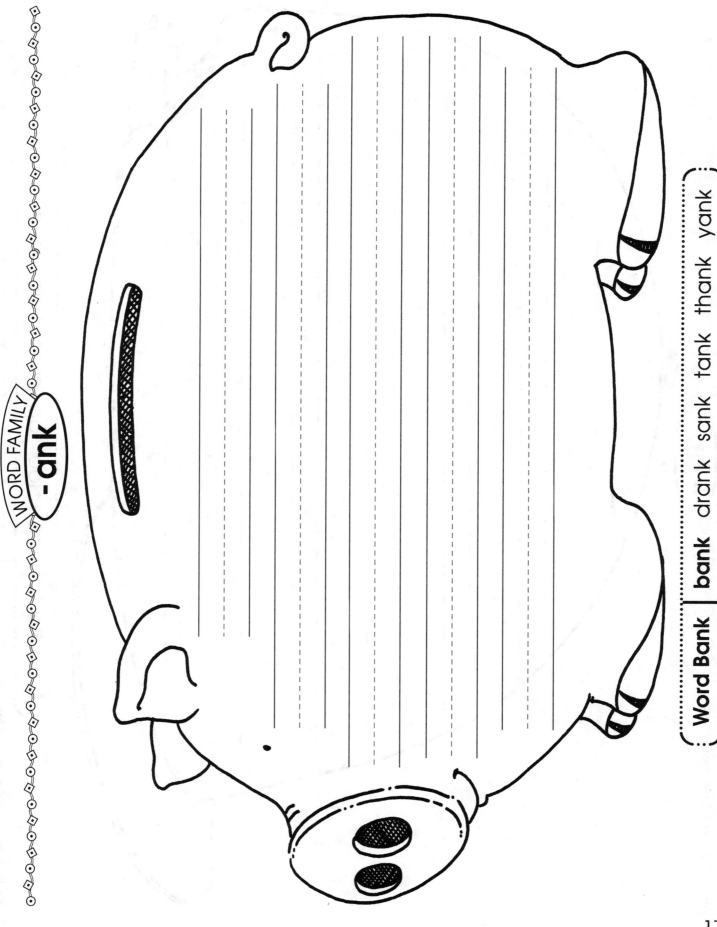

WORD FAMILY

-ank

Word Bank | **bank** drank sank tank thank yank

Word Family Stationery Scholastic Professional Books

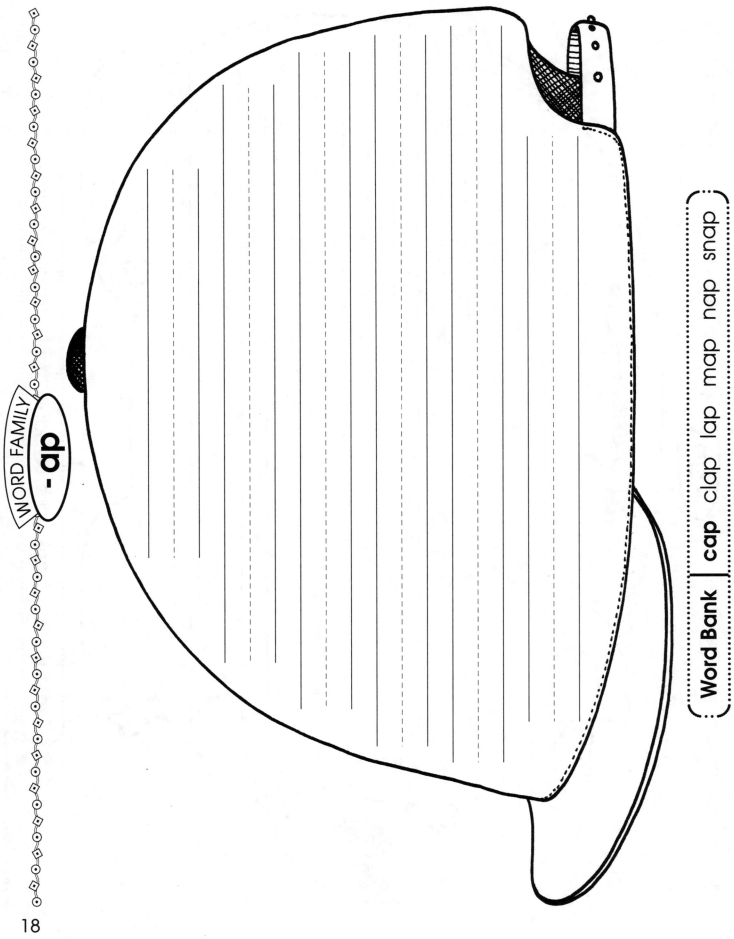

WORD FAMILY

-ap

Word Bank | **cap** clap lap map nap snap

Word Family Stationery Scholastic Professional Books

WORD FAMILY

-ape

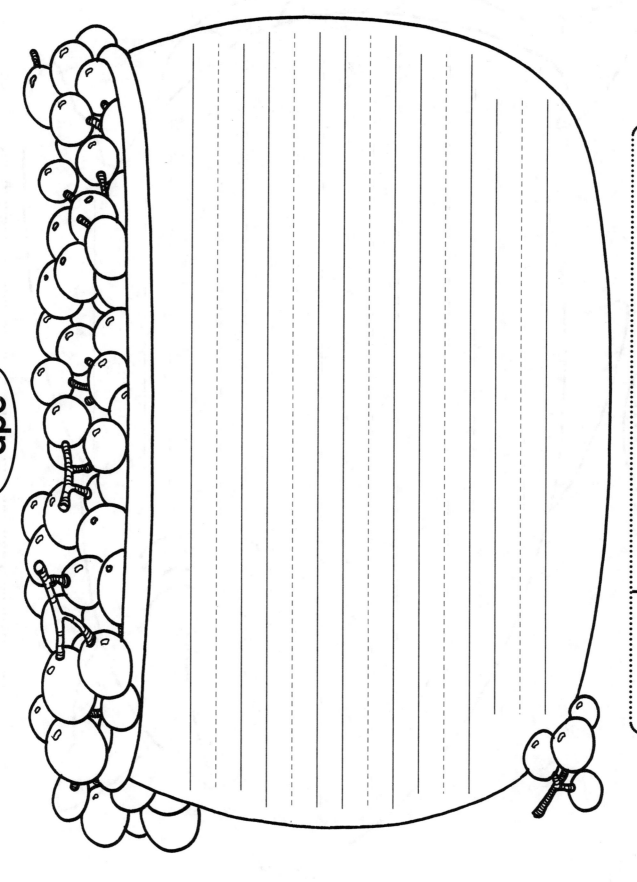

Word Bank | **grapes** ape cape drape shape tape

Word Family Stationery   Scholastic Professional Books

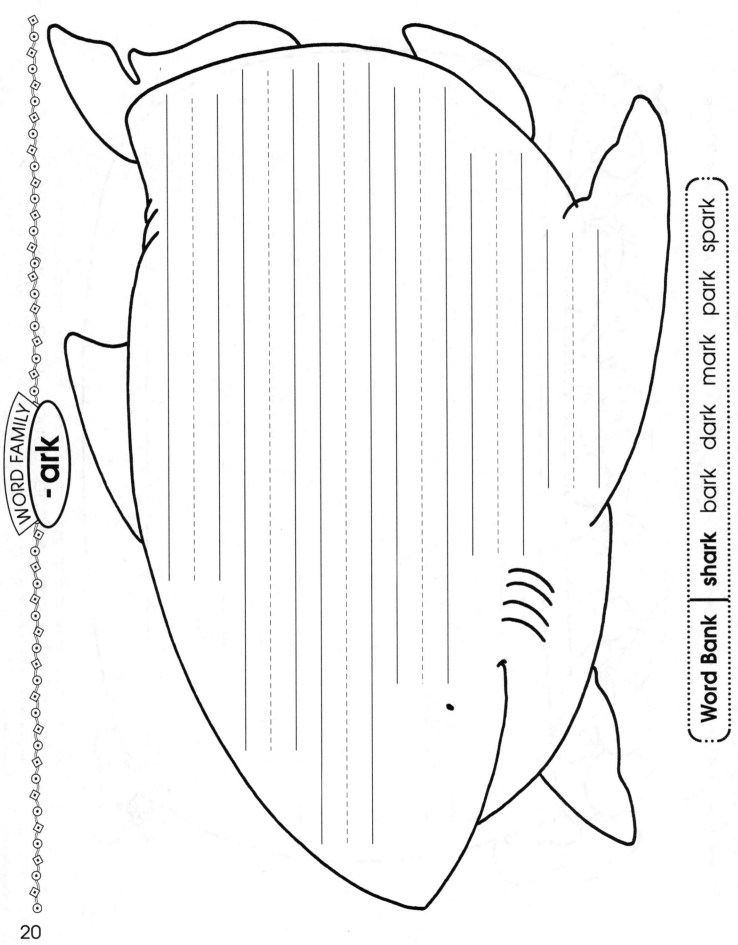

WORD FAMILY

-ark

Word Bank | **shark** bark dark mark park spark

Word Family Stationery Scholastic Professional Books

Word Bank | **trash** cash crash dash flash splash

Word Bank | **cat** bat hat rat sat that

Word Family Stationery   Scholastic Professional Books

Word Bank | **skate** date gate late plate state

Word Bank | **paw** claw draw jaw saw straw

Word Family Stationery   Scholastic Professional Books

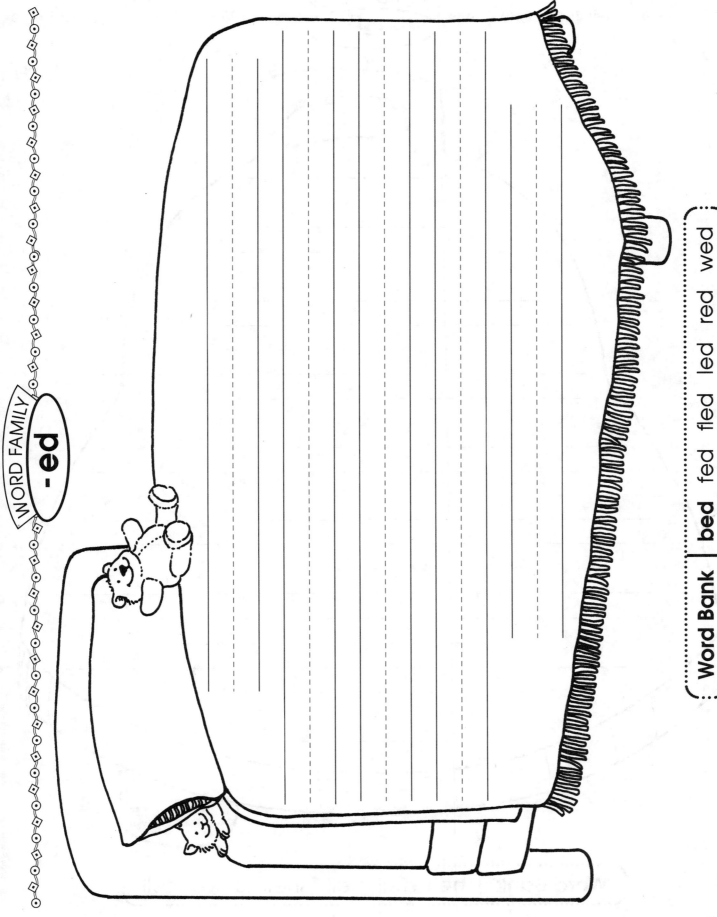

WORD FAMILY
-ed

Word Bank | **bed** fed fled led red wed

Word Family Stationery Scholastic Professional Books

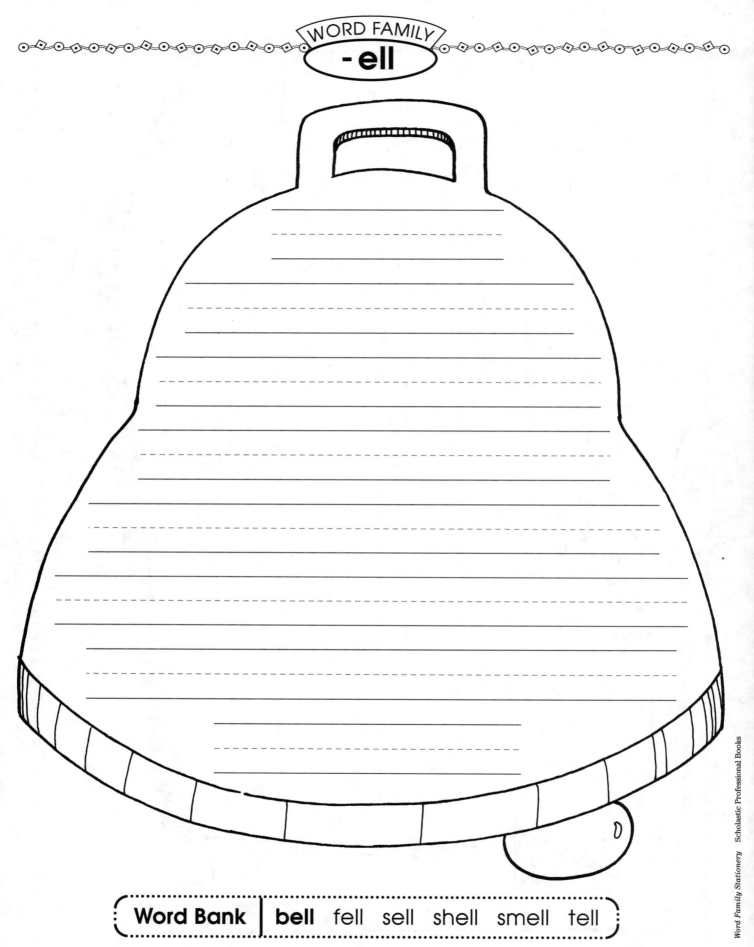

Word Bank | **bell** fell sell shell smell tell

Word Family Stationery   Scholastic Professional Books

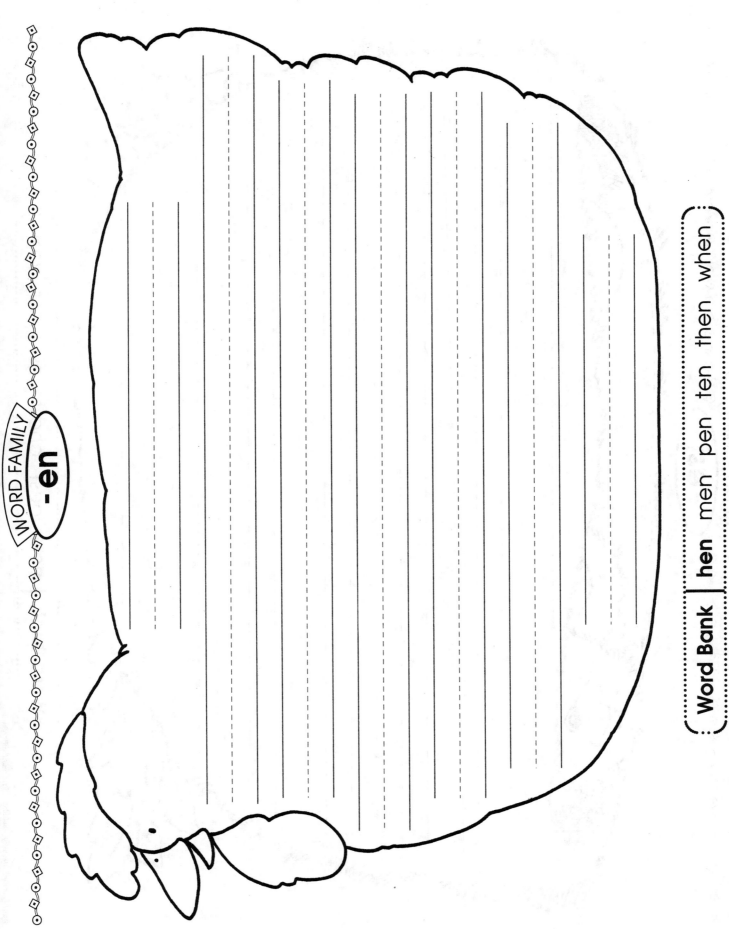

WORD FAMILY

-en

Word Bank | hen men pen ten then when

Word Bank | **nest** best chest rest test vest

Word Family Stationery Scholastic Professional Books

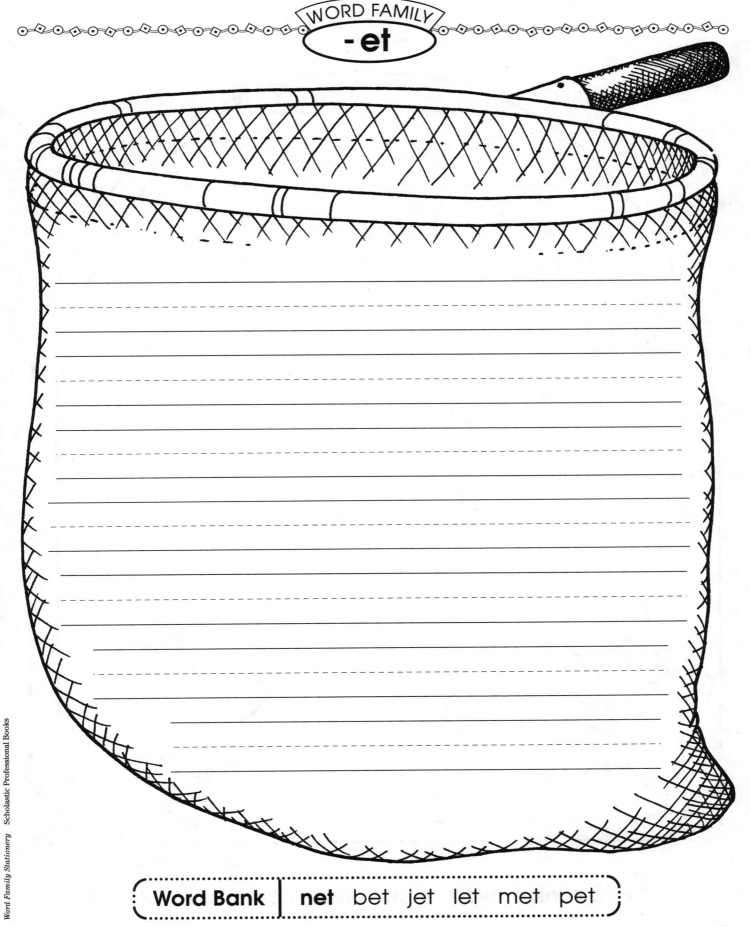

WORD FAMILY
-et

Word Bank | **net** bet jet let met pet

Word Bank | **mice** nice price rice slice twice

Word Family Stationery   Scholastic Professional Books

(lined writing space)

Word Bank | **chick** brick kick sick thick trick

Word Bank | **slide** bride hide ride tide wide

Word Family Stationery Scholastic Professional Books

Word Bank | **pin** fin grin spin twin win

Word Family Stationery Scholastic Professional Books

Word Family Stationery   Scholastic Professional Books

Word Bank | **pine** line mine nine shine vine

WORD FAMILY
-ing

Word Bank | **ring** king sing spring swing wing

36

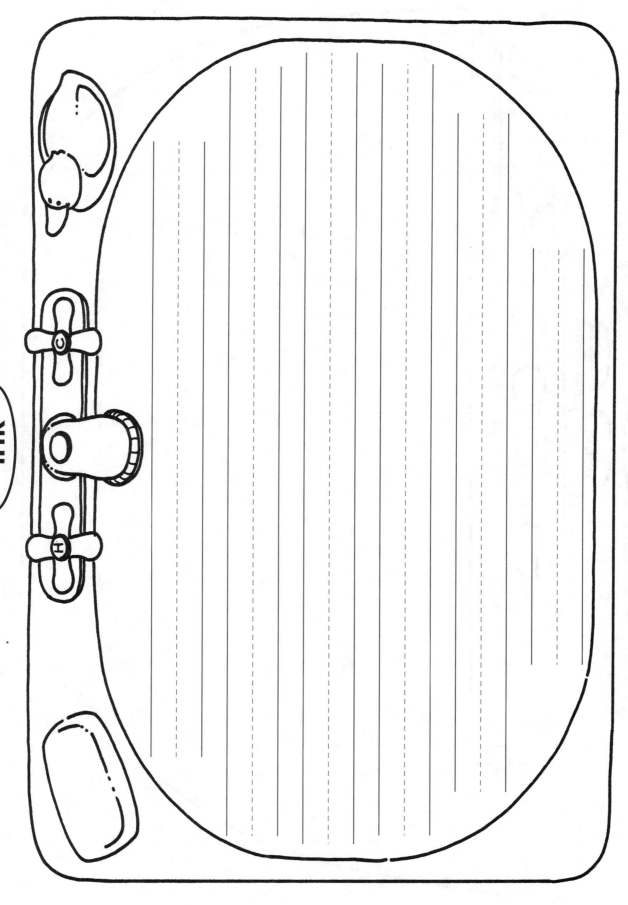

WORD FAMILY -ink

Word Bank | sink blink ink pink think wink

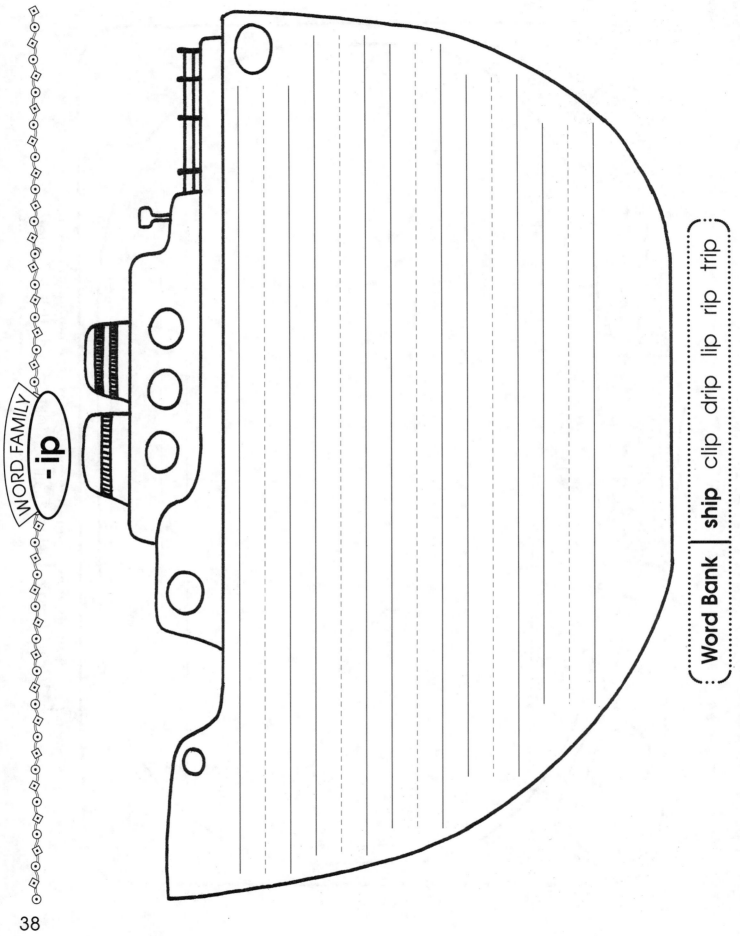

WORD FAMILY

-ip

Word Bank | **ship** clip drip lip rip trip

Word Family Stationery   Scholastic Professional Books

Word Bank | **sock** block clock dock lock rock

Word Family Stationery Scholastic Professional Books

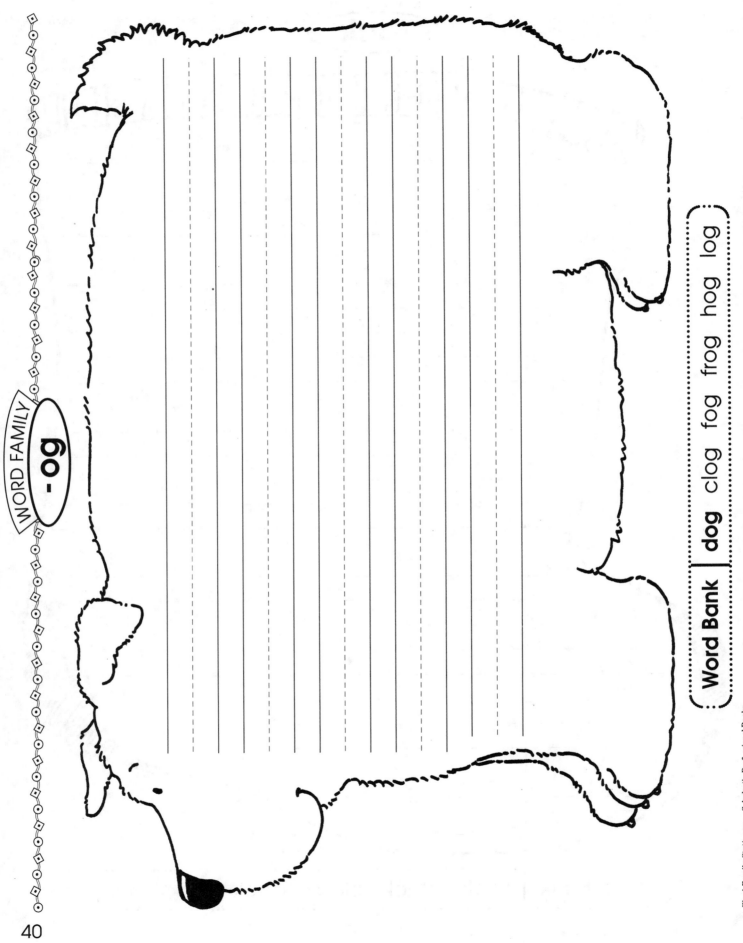

WORD FAMILY
-og

Word Bank | **dog** clog fog frog hog log

Word Family Stationery Scholastic Professional Books

Word Bank | **top** drop hop mop shop stop

WORD FAMILY

-ot

Word Bank | **pot** dot got hot knot spot

Word Family Stationery Scholastic Professional Books

WORD FAMILY -ub

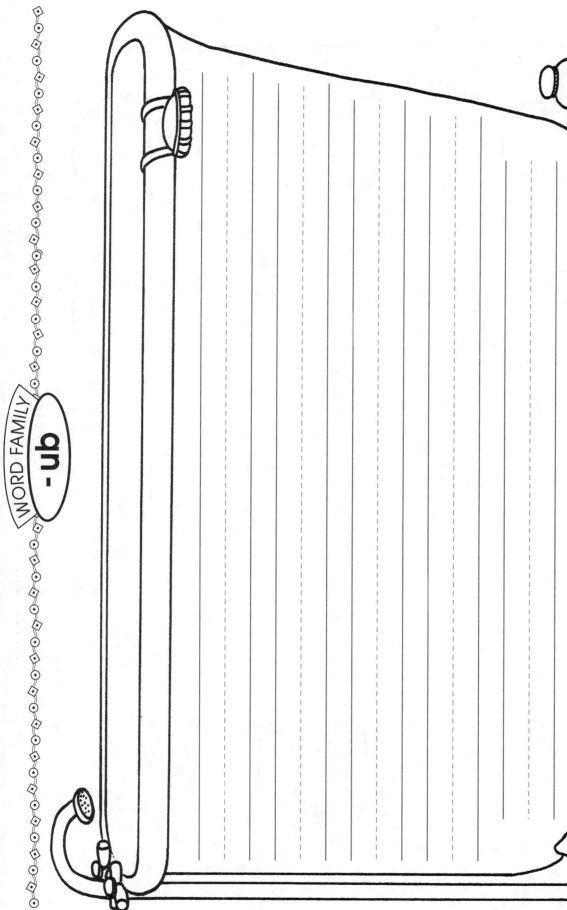

Word Bank | **tub** club cub stub sub rub

Word Family Stationery Scholastic Professional Books

43

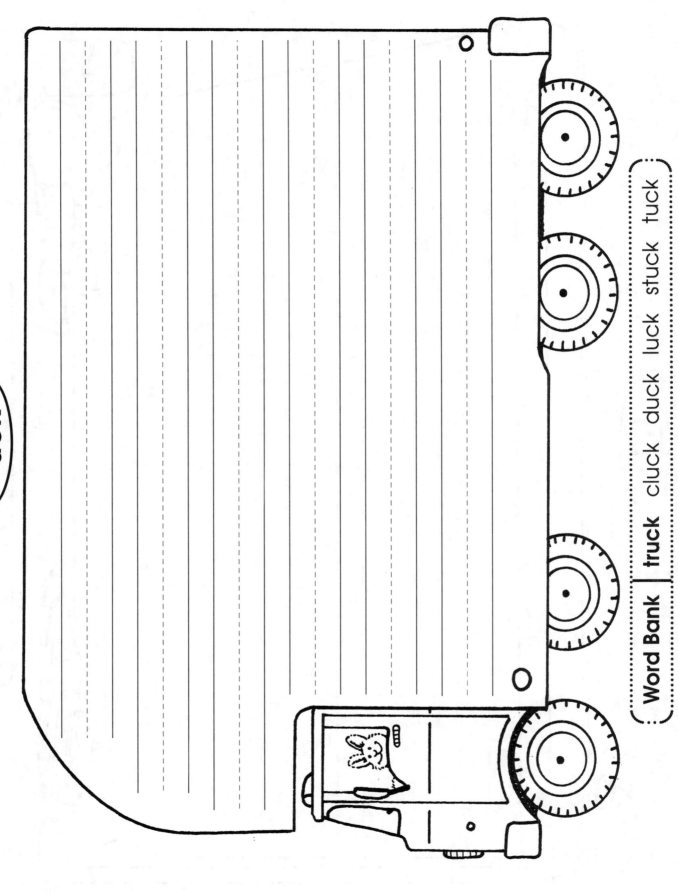

WORD FAMILY
-uck

Word Bank | truck cluck duck luck stuck tuck

Word Family Stationery   Scholastic Professional Books

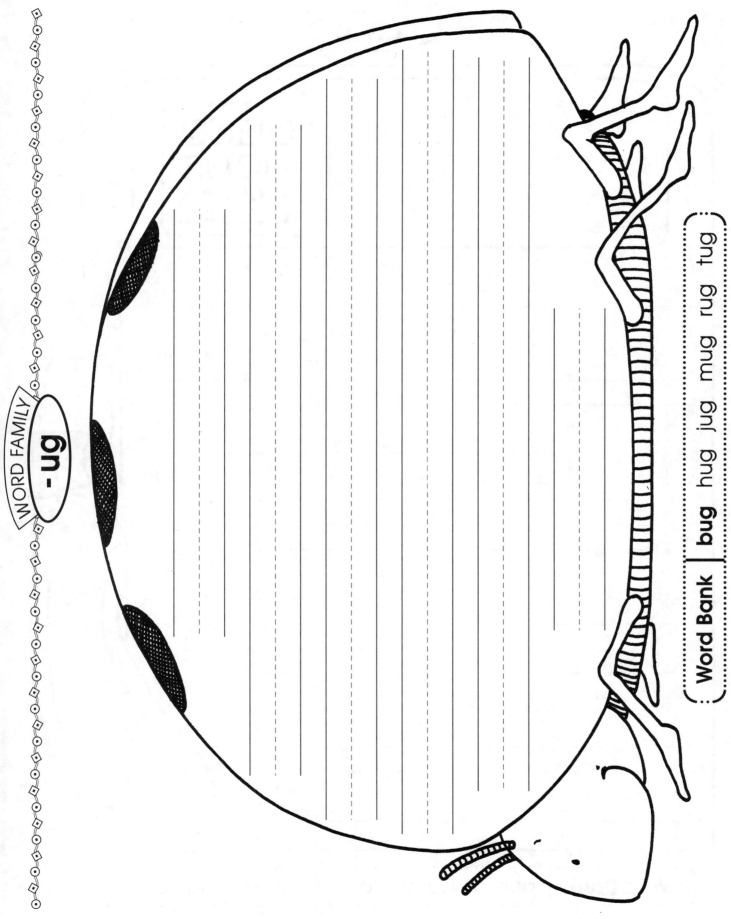

WORD FAMILY

-ug

Word Bank | **bug** hug jug mug rug tug

Word Family Stationery Scholastic Professional Books

$ 0 0 . 0 0

0 0 0 0

REGULAR
1 3 2 . 9

Word Bank | **pump** bump clump dump jump stump

Word Family Stationery   Scholastic Professional Books

WORD FAMILY

-unk

Word Bank | **skunk** bunk dunk junk sunk trunk

Word Family Stationery Scholastic Professional Books

47

WORD FAMILY

-ut

Word Bank | **nut** but cut hut rut shut